OVERCOMING SUPERHERO SYNDROME

LIVING BEYOND THE LABELS, EXPECTATIONS & IDENTITIES.

WHITNEY GILBERT

Copyright © 2023 Whitney Gilbert & Nap Rip Publishing

All rights reserved, including the right to reproduce this book or portions thereof in any form whatsoever by author. No part of this book may be reproduced, scanned, or distributed in any print or electric form without author's prior expressed written consent.

LIVING BEYOND THE LABELS, EXPECTATIONS & IDENTITIES

FOR MORE FROM

WHITNEY GILBERT

PLEASE VISIT

WWW.WHITNEYGILBERT.COM

FOREWORD

Each and every one of us has been given a natural gift for a divine reason. That talent, ability, or skillset is called a gift because it is recognized a present from God. Some aren't aware of their gifts and half of the people who find theirs, ultimately abandon them. Most will only use their gifts to benefit themselves, but something powerful happens when someone attaches their gift to a greater purpose to benefit others. It is the act of giving what was god given, back to God. This is what we are witnessing with this offering by Whitney Gilbert.

As a behavioral therapist and teacher, Whitney Gilbert has continually displayed an impressive level of consciousness and execution. From what I've seen with my own eyes, it's her mindset and intentions, accompanied by her ability to listen to understand and articulate to be understood, that fosters Whitney's high level of achieving the desired results.

If the "desired result" for this book is to end suffering and release the captives into the freedom and glory of their greater existence, I can only await the multitudes of testimonies that will undoubtedly come from this work. Bridging gaps that were once thought to be unable to be consolidated, is just another day at work for this amazing black woman.

Within these pages you will find golden nuggets of healing and wisdom that if properly invested, will certainly lead you to a true wealth of life.

BRIAN HYPPOLITE

DEDICATION

This book is dedicated to my parents, Angela and Bobby. They are two individuals who emerged from pasts filled with trauma and faced countless trials, yet found ways to make the most out of the lives they were given. Despite lacking examples of what a happy home should be, they made it their mission to provide us with the best opportunities for a life that would differ from theirs. I am immensely grateful for the wisdom they imparted upon me and the lessons I learned in embracing my own greatness through my experiences. They raised two remarkable young women, and though they may not have had the privilege of learning love in the ways they needed, they built a foundation based on their own understanding.

I would like to express my heartfelt gratitude to my sisters, Jillian and Kasandra, who continuously remind me of my potential and keep me motivated. Thank you for holding me accountable for the energy I embody, no matter how challenging it may have been. I deeply appreciate you for witnessing my transformation. This journey has not only enabled my personal growth but has also inspired an entire community of individuals to recognize their own greatness. You are embodiments of love, and I am eternally grateful for your presence in my life.

Next, I would like to acknowledge and thank Brian Hyppolite. You have been a true inspiration. From the day we crossed paths, you recognized a light within me and pushed me beyond my limits to keep it burning brightly. You helped me understand that regardless of the challenges life presents, my destiny surpasses anything standing in my way. Your creation of Manifest University has seamlessly complemented the work I undertake daily, and for that, I am forever indebted to you.

Last but certainly not least, I want to express my special thanks to Parenting with Purpose. I have had the privilege of hearing your stories and witnessing firsthand your growth and elevation on this journey of self-love and personal development. You motivate me to strive towards becoming an improved version of myself. May you continue to thrive as you spread awareness and love to all those you encounter. You are beacons of light shining brilliantly amidst the darkness.

TABLE OF CONTENTS

INTRODUCTION	**11**
Why Parent With Purpose	15
Breaking The Ice	19
CHAPTER ONE: Destroy and Rebuild	**21**
Children Lean From What They Experience	34
Steps To Processing Anger	36
How To Break Superhero Syndrome	46
Building Your Foundation	51
Setting Family Values	53
Goal Setting	57
Setting Boundaries	62
Setting A Foundation For Self-Esteem	73
CHAPTER 2: Taking Your Power Back	**79**
Evaluating Your Stress	80
Identifying Needs	92
Removing Anger	93
Accountability	98
Face Your Fears	111
Walking In Truth	113
Transparency Check	120
Speaking Life Into Yourself	125
Taking Action	127
Cultivating Your Environment	128
Evaluating Your Daily Task	135
CHAPTER 3 Building a Foundation	**138**
Communicating Effectively	140
What I Want For My Child	145
Reinforcement, Consequences, And Follow Through	149
CHAPTER 4: Grief	**167**
Understanding Grief & Overcoming Loss	168
Identifying the Stages of Grief	171
Eliminating The Why	179

The most precious gift any person is rewarded with is parenthood. There are many individuals who have never and will never get to experience this opportunity. You have been chosen. Embrace it as a blessing.

INTRODUCTION

My purpose in writing this book is to provide guidance on how to embrace truth and navigate life with love. We have allowed our surroundings and society to shape our perspective, but many of the examples we encounter are unrealistic and outdated. Throughout generations, we have witnessed families crumble due to a lack of understanding when it comes to the true essence of love. Our perception of love is often influenced by observing interpersonal relationships within our families or what we see on television and social media. However, love is experienced differently by everyone. It is our responsibility to embark on a personal journey of self-discovery, uncovering what truly ignites this feeling within us and how we can share it with others. Those who resist learning new ways to love are often trapped in survival mode.

Survival mode compels individuals to operate from a place of trauma and stress, causing them to act based on emotions rather than a clear state of mind. This can lead to reactive behavior, where past experiences dictate their present moments. These instinctive reactions feel almost involuntary, as if our bodies have a mind of their own. These moments have been deeply ingrained in our subconscious as fear-driven responses. However, when we connect with our present selves, we can align with less trauma and more self-love. Love encompasses far more than mere butterflies and red hearts. Love is about looking at yourself in the mirror, embracing your truest form without any pretenses or masks, and acknowledging the growth you have achieved. It requires a dedicated commitment to continuously learn new ways to love yourself each day.

By embarking on this journey of self-discovery and embracing the transformative power of love, we can truly experience a profound shift in our lives. In the pages that follow, I will provide insights, guidance, and practical tools to help you uncover the depths of your own love and radiate it outwards. Get ready to embark on a transformative path of self-love and genuine connection.

Say this out loud: *I am willing to consistently elevate my consciousness to align with the greatest version of myself!*

This book will guide you through a journey of loving yourself by embracing the truth. The tools you will gain will empower you as you learn to be your superhero. You will learn new information to help you and your family solve problems and effectively communicate in what most deem the most difficult of situations. I want you to understand that this process requires dedication and consistency. Learning to speak love can be compared to learning a foreign language which would require you to consciously practice it until you can do it fluently without thought.

"Overcoming Superhero Syndrome" is meant to help you pick up your power and walk in truth. It is time to focus your energy on pouring back into you. We have all been given individual powers which align with our purpose. Unfortunately, many people have adopted a mindset that tells us that your needs are no longer a priority because you are a parent. In our society, the idea that parenting is hard and overwhelming has been reinforced for generations. It has become normal for parents to struggle, and we often find comfort in bonding with other parents to continue supporting this outdated mindset. We have also learned that if we haven't experienced fulfillment, parenting will allow us to receive instant levels of validation. Children not only want our love and help but need it. However, we must accept that to be effective and align with our most authentic selves. It's time to start using our powers to help achieve our greatness.

WHY PARENT WITH PURPOSE

When I use the phrase parenting yourself with purpose, it simply means you are learning to identify with the adult version of yourself and no longer allowing the inner child to dictate how you should maneuver through life. They say a parent's responsibility is to bring up a child or raise them. When you have led a life of superhero syndrome, you may have been placed into an adult role but mentally still a child. This allows many people to become stuck in this space. Although our body has developed, our mental and emotional capacity still plays catch up. When embarking on this journey of self-healing, we are forced into some very uncomfortable spaces. I was often facing myself and the trauma I had experienced. I overcame prolonged bouts of depression, anxiety, suicidal ideations, burnout, sexual trauma, and homelessness. I felt alone, as though I had no one who truly understood what I was experiencing, and often this was very true. My main support systems were removed when I lost both of my parents within a span of two years. I felt completely broken and found myself overwhelmed by grief, operating from a place of scarcity. I was so consumed by my emotions that I failed to realize that I held the key to everything I believed I lacked.

When new problems arose, my inner child was the one who was crying out by not having her mother and father reassure her that everything was going to be ok. This journey took me almost 5 years to recover from, and I still have moments where my inner child wakes up and wants to take the light to shine on the parts of me that identify with brokenness. I've learned to acknowledge her, hug her, speak life into her, and then gently guide her back to a place of peaceful rest without disrupting the progress I have made. Throughout the years, I have encountered individuals who have taught me valuable life lessons. Many times, when faced with a problem, I was pushed into survival mode, which hindered my clarity. I found myself being pulled into a dark place, feeling myself falling and desperately shouting for someone to rescue me, but my grip was slipping away. That's what happens when you're in survival mode—it drags you into a space where you can barely hold on. This only leads to stress and heightened anxiety levels. The most effective way to overcome this stage is by understanding the purpose behind the problems you encounter. Here are a few questions to ask yourself during this time:

- Am I in survival mode? Do my instincts drive me to fight, run away, or immediately solve the problem I am facing?

- What am I supposed to learn from this experience?

With every problem comes a lesson. It is up to us to define what it is. You must be committed to finding solutions and not focusing on the problems.

Can You Be Committed to This Lifestyle?

Our jobs as parents are to teach our children how to maneuver through life by effectively using the knowledge we've gained over the years. We do this by being a mirror they can reflect upon. Many of us have struggled in silence on this journey because we allowed ourselves to focus on life's problems and not on how to identify solutions. Life will bring forth challenges, and it is up to us to decide how it will affect us. It is up to us to shift our consciousness which is done by aligning with truth and moving with a love of self. This allows you to fulfill your own needs. Once you start pouring into yourself, your cup will begin running over, leaving tiny trails everywhere you go. Without trying, you will create a fountain overflowing into the cups of your family, who will now begin creating an overflow of their own. This is the way we become the change our family needs.

When my mother was close to transitioning, she looked at me and said, "Look at you. So beautiful, so much life in you." She looked at me as if she was disgusted. I tried not to allow the statement to bother me, but it sat with me. Right before my mother became sick, she was CEO of her own non-profit, finally fulfilling a dream she had postponed for years. She had convinced herself that she had to wait until her children were old enough to provide for themselves for her to carry out her dreams. When she looked at me, she saw the opportunities she walked about from, the excuses and stories she made that stopped her from pursuing her goals. She convinced herself that being our mother and our superhero was her most important role. She lost her sense of self in the labels she was attached to. She never imagined that by saving herself and identifying with the truth, she would teach us to do the same.

BREAKING THE ICE

- Who are 5 people in your life you can call your superheroes? Or that you admire?
- If you had an opportunity to sit down with a younger version of yourself, what would be 5 things you would tell them?
- If you had to choose 3 words to describe yourself, what would they be?
- What are some things you wish your parents knew about you?
- How much time are you willing to devote to yourself for self-development?

- When did you feel safe enough to express your true feelings without judgment?
- If you could sit down and have a transparent conversation with your parents, what would you tell them you needed?
- How often do you hear words of affirmation from the people in your inner circle?

CHAPTER 1

Destroy and Rebuild

When you hear the term superhero, many of us picture some masked mystical figure dressed up in a costume showing up when others need to be saved. A Superhero's whole identity is wrapped up in sacrificing themselves to save others. Although most of the superheroes we have encountered have been fictional, many of us have adopted this same identity. We have allowed ourselves to receive validation from saving those in our lives while neglecting our own personal needs. While there is nothing wrong with helping our loved ones, we must understand it is not our job to save the people we love. We can only walk with them and share with them the knowledge we have gained while on our own independent journey.

Taking on the role of a savior or superhero keeps us from aligning with ourselves and hinders our loved ones from learning to problem-solve effectively. In the role of a parent, we often believe that our primary purpose is to shield our children from harm. We strive to catch them before they fall and soften the blow when they experience failure. While all of these aspects are undoubtedly important, we often overlook the most crucial factor: teaching them how to rise again after each setback.

A common phrase heard from parents is, 'Be careful!' This phrase immediately triggers fear in their minds. Instead, we should focus on teaching our children to be mindful, encouraging them to assess their surroundings and make informed decisions based on their observations. When we fail to give our children tools to help them maneuver through life, we set them up for failure. We must also keep in mind that our children were given free will to choose how they will use the knowledge given to them. Although they may have the tools in hand, they may make decisions that don't align with what they have been taught. This does not mean you have failed or the foundation you have built is weak. Use these moments as teaching opportunities between you.

Are You Living as A Superhero?

There are various paths that can lead to the development of a superhero identity. For many, it can be traced back to a time when they or someone they loved felt unsafe within their own home. This experience may have left them feeling guilty for lacking the means to protect themselves or their loved ones, resulting in a sense of helplessness. Conversely, for some individuals, this dynamic may have been reversed. Their parents may have experienced trauma long before their arrival, failing to address and heal from it. Unknowingly, these parents projected unrealistic expectations onto their children, seeking to fill the void they felt within themselves. Such relationships often foster codependency.

If you have been a caregiver to someone who was ill or have taken care of someone with special needs, you may also be familiar with the phenomenon known as superhero syndrome. We find solace in knowing that we can assist these individuals as they rely on our support. We tell ourselves phrases like, 'They need me,' 'They can't do this without me,' or 'Who else will do it?' The validation we receive within this role encourages us to continue prioritizing the needs of others, often at the expense of our own well-being, which becomes increasingly distant from our field of vision.

Superhero syndrome can also be associated with a term I have heard called parentification. Parentification can be used to describe how a parent influences a child to take on adult roles and responsibilities. Superhero parents often produce parentified children. The children in this scenario may often feel obligated to adopt this identity. Parents suffering from superhero syndrome will often seek help from their children to maintain a balance within themselves and their environment. In my home, my parents experienced years of trauma before my birth. My mother called me her angel and stated I was sent here to save her. She said that without me, she wouldn't have survived the path she was on. She said my birth gave her a reason to love life. When those moments of happiness left her, I made it my duty to help them reemerge.

In parentification, we want to see our parents happy, so we often follow through with anything they ask of us, even if it doesn't align with our needs. Children still have trouble identifying our needs, it is easier to identify with those being articulated to us. We watch our parents become overwhelmed and burnt out by life. Children want to do anything to see the joy on their parent's faces, so they volunteer to do anything to lighten the load. Some children begin to take on the identity of a missing parent or significant other to give the love their parent is missing. This can lead to overwhelming emotions a child may have trouble processing. Many will internalize them, keeping them tucked away in their subconscious mind. This is one of the leading factors of superhero syndrome.

Children are extremely aware of our emotions. They align with our frequencies by using nonverbal communication. Their first interactions with us were based on modeling and identifying needs without words. We must be mindful that while our children will instantly give us validation, their responsibility is not to comfort us in this space. It is the job of the parent or adult to heal themselves from the parts of them they deem broken. It is much easier to blame someone else for the pain we experience instead of seeing how we play a role in our own suffering. While we may not have been the cause of the pain, it is our responsibility to heal from it.

During my journey, I found. It was so easy to blame another individual for not being what I needed them to be instead of growing into who I was meant to be. I allowed my light to burn bright enough to lead the way for others but become dim when it was my turn. I began finding comfort in the darkness. I adopted a mindset that led to me pretending I didn't care if I received help and would instead attempt to do everything myself. I was so stuck in living in the past that I turned down help convincing myself that I would be let down. I reflected on times in my childhood when asking for help made me feel more uncomfortable than going without it. I quickly learned that by making this choice, I put myself in so many difficult situations that could have been avoided. I forced myself into a world full of chaos that caused stress and anxiety to become my best friend. I allowed myself to become a victim of my own choices. This caused me to lower my frequency of accepting things and energies that didn't align with my purpose.

In many cases, this is when survival mode is activated. Humans have a hunger to belong and to feel love. When this need is not being met your energy will draw in others that will allow this part of you to become fed. Individuals who need love will become drawn to your light like a moth to a flame. This leads to you being distracted from giving your energy towards your true focus. These individuals meet all the criteria for those we deem broken, making us feel needed and validated.

When your role involves parenting a child and you are searching for fulfillment, your call is answered much more frequently. The need to solve all your children's problems becomes natural to you. This is how many codependent relationships are developed.

Codependent relationships can be extremely destructive to each party involved. You begin to feed the narrative that without you, the other party won't be able to accomplish things independently. You begin to develop unexpressed fears that can lead to a need to take full control. My codependent relationship began with me fulfilling a role for my mother. She always stated how much she needed me to show up for her and guilted me when I chose myself. She set the foundation for a love that was now filled with dysfunction. I struggled after her passing. I wanted to blame her, but I had to understand where she came from and what she endured. She was doing the best she could with the tools she was given. It was my job to release this false standard of love I was so familiar with.

Love is not defined by what you can do for someone, but rather by the relationship you have with yourself, which enables your love to be received and appreciated by others. Love should not be conditional. In my journey of understanding the true meaning of love, I realized that the role I played in her life, and the lack of healthy boundaries, led to dysfunctional dynamics in future relationships. When it is time for a past version of you to die, life will present you with familiar situations meant to bring you back to rekindle the spark that is slowly fizzling out. It is your job to decide whether you will move forward or become sucked back into the past version of yourself.

The first sign of you walking in familiar territory is that it will seem calm but quickly turn sour when your or your partner's needs aren't met. This triggers fight-or-flight responses. One party may run to avoid conflict to feel protected, while the other may need to roar loudly to scare off any opposing threat or simply be heard. The cycle will once again start over until one of you becomes exhausted. Many will have trouble articulating their emotions and feelings in these situations because they fear what the outcome of their expression will lead to. Although you know your expression may be needed, your fear of rejection by the other party often will outweigh your need to communicate. This often leads to a person feeling as though their voice is invalid. It is easy for us to identify that this behavior began in childhood. However, we overlook that this mindset is being reflected in our homes with our children.

You repeat what you don't heal. This is where you begin to see children act out to gain your attention in other ways. I recently did a listening test for several people where I asked specific questions about how they engaged with other adults in conversation. Many of them said they give their undivided attention to others while engaging. They stated that ignoring them would be rude, and they couldn't imagine behaving that way when someone was speaking to them. I then asked if the same behavior was reflected when speaking to their children. Their faces quickly changed as they admitted they had not given their children the same respect. We often don't realize that how we respond to our children is based on how our parents responded to us during childhood. Many of the responses come second nature flowing out of our mouths without giving them a second thought. This is why learning to reflect is so important. When we have heightened responses to our children's negative behavior, we reinforce it to become more frequent. We can shift behavior by using emotional intelligence when reacting to them.

*Answer the following questions below.

• Ask yourself how often you feel the need to be in control of the outcome with your child?

_____

_____

_____

_____

• What steps do you take to control disagreements with your children?

_____

_____

_____

_____

_____

• How do you and your significant other handle disagreements in front of your children?

_____

_____

_____

_____

_____

_____

_____

_____

• Do you feel the need to use corporal punishment when disciplining your children? Do you feel you have accomplished your goal after reacting this way? How do you reconnect with your children afterwards? How do you feel emotionally after this interaction?

_____

_____

_____

_____

_____

_____

• How do your children respond to this type of discipline?

_____

_____

_____

_____

_____

_____

_____

- When you are done discipling your children, how do you and your partner/co-parent work together to strategize for future obstacles?

_____

_____

_____

_____

_____

CHILDREN LEARN FROM WHAT THEY EXPERIENCE

When parenting yourself, learning what emotions you are battling with will allow you to evaluate what you are experiencing more clearly. This is what we call conscious parenting. This enables us to be mindful of our present state of being and the needs of the child before embarking on active problem-solving. This helps us to identify whether we are holding anger within ourselves. We often don't realize that we have been carrying this energy.

Let's break this down with a few questions:

- Is there something you are currently angry about?
- Who or what is the cause of your anger?
- Are you unhappy with your current state of living? What would you change?
- Is there someone you feel has let you down? Why?
- Were you able to stand up for yourself or voice how you felt?
- In what ways would you like to feel more supported?
- What can you do to help you focus more on solutions than the problems you face?

-Now look at your answer to question 2, "What is the cause of your anger?" When evaluating our anger, we must remember that we are responsible for how we process it. This goes back to understanding the difference between being reactive and reflective. Reactions happen when we don't take the time to allow our initial emotions to process. We project the first surfaced level of emotion we feel. When you operate from reflection, you take time to pause before allowing your emotion to cause a reaction. You ask yourself questions such as: What is the truth in this situation? How can you focus on the solution and not the problem?

STEPS TO PROCESSING ANGER

- **Take a time out**: walk away if needed.
- **Establish a connection**: Remind yourself you are not your emotions, and they do not control you.
- **Fight the problem, not the person.**
- **Focus on solutions.**

One of the reasons why many of us face challenges with discipline is due to the conditioning that children are possessions to be controlled. It is crucial to shift this narrative. Children come through us; they do not belong to us. We are meant to teach them by mirroring behaviors we want them to display. It is also our job to teach them what an important role they play in the family dynamic. You do this by teaching them family values. Your values are the blueprints that reflect much of what we have learned in childhood. Children learn from what they experience. The intimate relationships we witnessed in childhood taught us our values about love and discipline. If your family believed in using physical force to disciple in your home, then, as a result, you may have done the same with your children.

If you are silenced when expressing yourself, you may struggle to set appropriate boundaries with individuals for fear of negative consequences.

Many of us who have experienced childhood trauma have learned to seek validation from those we care about. Some would label this as codependency. Much like superheroes, codependent individuals seek validation from their loved ones to give them a sense of self-worth. Codependency can cause a child to become terrified at the thought of being abandoned or rejected. This prompts individuals to place barriers around themselves for protection. Subconsciously, we create identities that surface when we need to feel safe. These types of relationships result in individuals overextending themselves to complete tasks that cause burnout. When an individual experiences burnout, they can't process their emotions effectively, leading to reactive responses instead of reflective ones. Some of us have learned to pretend to have a careless opinion because we anticipate our support will leave. This can lead to complete chaos. These types of codependent relationships can be detrimental to both parties. Unacknowledged fears that the codependent individual shares often lead to controlling and self-centered behaviors. These behaviors can warp the relationships between children and parents for generations. Fears such as these begin to surface in both our romantic relationships and those we have with our children. We often suppress these emotions each time they resurface. To heal from them, they must be addressed and released.

In the section below, rate these items on a scale of 1-10.

How often do you feel...?

- Angry 1 2 3 4 5 6 7 8 9 10
- Disappointed 1 2 3 4 5 6 7 8 9 10
- Fear 1 2 3 4 5 6 7 8 9 10
- Guilt 1 2 3 4 5 6 7 8 9 10
- Loneliness 1 2 3 4 5 6 7 8 9 10
- Blame yourself 1 2 3 4 5 6 7 8 9 10
- Numb 1 2 3 4 5 6 7 8 9 10
- Disconnected 1 2 3 4 5 6 7 8 9 10

Now, look at your responses. Circle any of the examples where you have scored 5 or higher and write your responses to the following questions.

1. Which of these do you have the highest score?

2. Is there a specific memory that has triggered this response?

- Anger: What benefit does holding on to anger have for you? Does the experience help you move towards a solution or keep you trapped in your emotions? Who else is affected by your holding on to this anger?

- Disappointment: Is this a feeling we want to continue experiencing? Have you placed unrealistic expectations on yourself or others, leading to this disappointment? What things can you do to minimize this experience in the future?

- Fear: What am I afraid of? What outcome am I trying to protect myself from? Am I afraid of being wrong? What things can go right if I release this fear?
- Guilt: Can you change what has already happened? What way can you better prepare in the future for when things don't go as planned?
- Loneliness: Have you isolated yourself from others? Have you convinced yourself that you don't need anyone due to your experiences? What steps have you taken to increase your support system? What other things in your life deserve your attention?

By holding on to anger we are reflecting this same behavior to our children. Children watch everything we do and apply these same behaviors to their lives. Have you ever observed your children playing with one another and heard them respond the very same way you have when discipling them? Although we have set values and goals with them we live by the standards that we have set in order for it to be reinforced with our loved ones. When we identify our triggers and work on releasing them, when we allow them to see the importance of facing our anger.

Your job is to help your child cultivate the environment that allows them to flourish. You are a contractor hired by the divine to use your knowledge and life experience to bring this new being's creations to fruition. The first step to doing this is by releasing the idea that you are the owner of this structure you've been gifted. In this relationship, you are working to build your child a strong foundation with the lessons you teach them over the years. The foundation of a structure is the most important because it dictates how long a structure can withstand the natural elements sent to weaken it. When parenting with purpose, you must set out to be intentional by creating values that align with your family. This is how you cultivate the environment you seek.

What's Behind Your Mask?

What are you hiding from? When things in life begin to feel overwhelming, we begin losing sight of ourselves. We attempt to suppress the feelings we are experiencing. This allows us to move through our day-to-day life without identifying a problem or finding a real solution. It is easier to pretend a problem doesn't exist than look it in the face. We often engulf ourselves in caring for others which often validates the story we have created. This type of behavior can lead to toxic connections. While instant gratification is received, it can have negative effects due to suppressed emotions. This is where we often see resentment of others. Our loved ones become the target of our lack of boundaries and ability to pour into ourselves. We even have unclear expectations for them to see how overwhelmed we are and grow upset when they don't notice. How can we expect others to empathize with us when we aren't being honest with ourselves? This is what society has shown us is the norm. Although this may seem like the most obvious reason to find a solution, many take it as another opportunity to avoid their own reality.

Behavior Check

- How has this behavior pattern helped or hindered you?

_____

_____

_____

_____

- What problems have you had to face due to your not following through with your needs?

_____

_____

_____

_____

- How has pretending that your needs weren't important caused you to have more stress?

_____

_____

_____

_____

- How can you begin prioritizing your needs?

_____

_____

_____

_____

If an abundance of joy has not been flowing through your life, then it's time to make a change. This is a decision that only you have the power to change. Are you ready to stand in your power? Are you willing to remove the identities you aligned with that caused you to make excuses and not move into action?

Breaking the Cycle

Healing from past pain requires you to release resentment and anger towards yourself and others. In Brian Hyppolite's book, Manifesting You, 111 Keys to Unlocking Your Divinity, he states that an angry heart is mad at itself. Mad at itself for allowing you to continue placing yourself in spaces that don't nurture or feed it the way it deserves. How dare you continue robbing yourself of the love you've been waiting for. Are you going to continue being a walking contradiction stating that you deserve love but turning your head and slapping it away each time it is presented to you? It is time to decide that you are worthy of the love you've been giving to others.

HOW TO BREAK SUPERHERO SYNDROME

In order to break free from superhero syndrome, you must focus your energy on a target for the future. You are beginning to move into unfamiliar territory; therefore, you will need to put some steps in place to help you achieve your greatness. Two things that will work as blueprints for your foundation are goals and values. Goals are determined by deciding what you want for yourself and your family. In my parenting classes, I ask, what is your end goal, or where do you see your family in the future? This helps you and your family to align your behaviors and daily practices with your goals.

Think of yourself as the contractor for your family's legacy. What types of material will you need to make a strong foundation that will weather the many storms to come? When most people make a goal, they think big and then become discouraged when things don't work out as they thought. Goal setting is about starting small and making attainable steps to complete daily. The large goal can still be your focus, but there are several steps to accomplish before reaching it. Choose something you can see yourself accomplishing within the next three months. This should be meaningful to you and will help you stay motivated in your daily execution. How will achieving this goal help your family have a better foundation for the future?

We often think that when we set goals, execution solely falls on us, and we often don't ask for help during the process. This is a sure way to set yourself up for failure. Asking for support to help you achieve your goal is necessary to help you gain the momentum to move forward. Superhero syndrome has taught us that asking for help will have a negative outcome; therefore, we have piled on countless amounts of work and struggled to get just one task done. When completing the activity "How to nurture a child" in the parenting workbook, you were able to select several characteristics you wanted to see in your child. Would you add suffering to that list? If the answer is no, then it's also time to remove it from your list. Learning to parent your children with purpose is also learning to parent yourself.

You are the reflection your child will see daily, so mirror behaviors you want them to immolate. Make a list of resources and support you can utilize to help you during this process. This can be family members, friends, neighbors, google, library, support groups, etc. This is the time to allow your voice to be heard.

You've spent years catering to everyone around you. This is the time to speak loudly for your own needs. A small portion of time should be dedicated to your goal each day. This will help you stay within the time frame allotted for completion. Understand that time frames can and should be evaluated if they seem unrealistic. Do not become discouraged. This is a sign that your goal may need to be broken down into smaller steps.

BUILDING YOUR FOUNDATION

The patterns of how we function in life are developed in our childhood. In fact, we learn who we believe we are and how the world around us functions by what our caregivers mirrored for us during our early years. You are in an amazing space to start fresh, wiping the slate clean by building a new foundation.

In Hindi, the word foundation is described as the act of starting something new or the fundamental assumptions from which something is developed. Whether building a structure or cultivating a new environment for yourself and your family to thrive, you must start by rewriting the foundation for long-lasting support. You are the innovator your family's legacy has been waiting for. You embarked on this journey because you were tired of the outdated mindsets within your family. It is time to do the unthinkable by showing your family they deserve more. To establish this foundation, there are several steps that can help you achieve long- lasting results. The first step is to define an end goal for your family, outlining how you envision their functioning. If the objective is to foster a life of wholeness and cultivate harmonious relationships among family members, it is essential to establish a set of values that align with this mindset. To accomplish this, collaborate with your loved ones to create a list of values that will serve as a guiding compass, keeping you focused on the desired outcome. Consider these values as the blueprint for success, as they will remind you of the expected behavior and how alignment with these values will manifest within your family.

SETTING FAMILY VALUES

Creating your family values will help to align with your family's purpose. This list will serve as a template to help guide you to walking out your family vision. It is easy to become distracted by the many obstacles life will present you with if you don't have something to remind you of the goal you are constantly working towards as a team. When creating this list, each family member must be able to discuss what is important to them. This allows everyone to take ownership in upholding these guidelines because they were able to participate in the creation. Many families have stated they have values they follow but have never discussed them. Instead, there is an assumption they should be known and understood. However, in numerous cases, we have witnessed children veering off in completely different directions simply because certain topics were not openly discussed.

If our intention is to instill new ways of communication, we must provide them with the opportunity to openly and honestly discuss various subjects with us, leaving no room for confusion. This approach serves as an excellent way to open the door for future conversations, even those that may involve uncomfortable topics.

The list should include things that are expected of **ALL** family members, such as

- Appropriate behaviors
- Consequences for behaviors that don't align with values and goals
- Love
- Views on spirituality
- Sex/ Relationships
- Quality time
- Money management
- Household responsibilities
- Education

Your list can include a few other topics, but these will work as the core for a successful foundation.

Discovering your Family's Values

Each family member (including your children) must contribute to answering each of the questions.

1. What are the expectations for respect from others in your home? (Ex: speaking calmly when talking to each other or using kind language)

_____

_____

_____

_____

_____

2. What are the current consequences of not being respectful?

_____

_____

_____

_____

3. Do your actions align with your intentions to create a safe and whole environment for your family?

_____

_____

_____

_____

_____

4. Do you take accountability for your actions? Why or why not? How can you make a better effort when following through with this?

_____

_____

_____

_____

_____

_____

5. How open-minded are you to criticism from others? What steps can you take to become more open to receiving feedback?

_____

_____

_____

_____

_____

6. When you were a child, what activities did you enjoy using your creativity? How can you use those creative traits when teaching your children?

_____

_____

_____

_____

_____

7. How important is education in your home? Why? When answering this question, ask yourself are you projecting your expectations on your children to fulfill a path you chose not to complete?

_____

_____

_____

_____

_____

8. How often should you implement fun and leisure activities within your family schedule? What types of activities do you enjoy?

_____

_____

_____

_____

_____

9. What are your spiritual beliefs? How do you intend to educate your child about your version of spirituality?

_____

_____

_____

_____

_____

10. How comfortable are you speaking about sex in your home as a family? What are some ways to openly discuss without imposing your own bias?

_____

_____

_____

_____

_____

11. What is your relationship with money? Do you consider yourself good at attracting abundance? If not, are you comfortable asking for guidance/assistance? What has stopped you from getting help?

_____

_____

_____

_____

_____

12. What are your expectations for honesty in your home? What are the consequences of not being honest?

_____

_____

_____

_____

_____

_____

GOAL SETTING

Setting goals is essential when building a strong foundation for your family. It is far easier to achieve your goals when doing it as a family unit. It allows you to bond together by focusing on a common desire. Now that you have established your values together, your goals should align with what you want to see in the future.

Mapping Out Your Plan

• What do you want to accomplish within the next 6-9 months? (Ex: starting a new business, teaching my child to read, purchasing a car, planning a family vacation).

_____

_____

_____

_____

_____

- Why is this important to you?

_____

_____

_____

- What strengths and resources do you have access to help you accomplish this?

_____

_____

_____

_____

- What obstacles could interfere with you accomplishing this goal?

_____

_____

_____

_____

- What will happen if you follow through with your goal?

_____

_____

_____

_____

- Who will support and encourage you as you walk out of your goals?

_____

_____

_____

_____

_____

_____

- What is a goal your entire family can work on together?

_____

_____

_____

_____

When goal setting, it is important to start with a big goal and then break it down into smaller time frames. This allows it to become more attainable. Many people struggle with successfully accomplishing their goals due to not breaking them down properly. A big goal can become more intimidating especially when small progress is not being noted appropriately. Small victories keep us motivated to push forward towards our large goals. If you find yourself overwhelmed or not making progress it may be time to reevaluate your goal by breaking it down into smaller steps or time frames.

Now that you have created a BIG goal to be accomplished in 6-9 months, let's break this down into smaller steps. Below list steps you must take in order to achieve your goal within the next 90 days.

_____

_____

_____

_____

_____

_____

What are some steps you can accomplish within the next 30 days to help further this process?

_____

_____

_____

_____

_____

What steps can you accomplish weekly/ daily to help your goal become reality?

_____

_____

_____

_____

_____

Set a clear and measurable deadline for each goal. Each weekly follow up with your goals to monitor your progress. This also allows you to evaluate whether your deadline needs to be shifted. Record your progress on your goals.

SETTING BOUNDARIES

Boundaries are essential when setting a new standard in your home. They help to determine what you are willing and not willing to tolerate from others. By setting boundaries for those in your life, you are setting guidelines for how you are allowing others to treat you. When you don't set clear boundaries, it is easy for others to manipulate you into doing things that don't align with you. This is imperative if you have struggled with your self-esteem. Low self- esteem can cause you to feel as though you deserve to be disrespected or not deserve better.

You may look at yourself and say this doesn't apply to me because I feel confident. When you look at yourself in the mirror, you love who you see, but it doesn't stop there. Your self-esteem level is the way you view yourself subconsciously. It may be how you sabotage yourself from new opportunities by talking yourself out of it. You may tell yourself the timing isn't right instead of taking the proper steps to follow through with preparation. You freeze when given a new opportunity. This is a reason setting boundaries for yourself is important. For you to work on becoming the best part of yourself, having boundaries in place for others will allow you time to walk out the things necessary to achieve your own greatness.

Superhero syndrome has taught us that we need validation from others to feel better about ourselves when we should be the ones giving ourselves the validation. Validation comes from standing in your power, walking out your goals in real-time, and removing fear from your subconscious. We have been programmed to feel validated by performing for individuals in our lives. We choose to allow them to trample over our boundaries because we fear losing them. Although we don't know that standing in our power will cause this response, we allow it to paralyze us.

We would rather deal with the recurring trauma that comes with being used than set a boundary that will allow us to flourish in ways we could have never imagined. Some fear the responsibility of achieving something because accountability would make us feel trapped. We spend so much time giving to others that we feel guilty about caring for ourselves. We convince ourselves that without us, others are helpless.

This allows our actions to become quickly rooted in fear. You may be in fear of:

- Their emotional response or reaction = lack of protection
- What this person's life will look like without your guidance = lack of control
- Where you will find the validation you have received from them in the past = lack of self
- How your family will be affected by your choice = lack of clarity
- Failure

You are learning to take your power back by setting appropriate boundaries for yourself. To continue moving in a way that best serves you, you must communicate what you are not willing to put up with anymore. The past version of yourself struggled with saying no for fear that it would cause division and create an unhealthy relationship with those around you.

Take a moment to ask, how harmonious has your life been by allowing others to walk all over you while you laid your power down? Were you fulfilled in those moments, or were you living in constant regret? Have you been holding on to your anger?

Saying no does not make you a bad person. You don't have to aggressively yell no to your friends and family when they ask you something. You have to be willing to say no to what doesn't align with you. You should not have to apologize for speaking up about what you are uncomfortable with. You are not responsible for anyone else's feelings. You are only responsible for speaking the truth. Living in truth allows you to immediately identify when you are out of alignment with your goals. When we are out of alignment, we attract unmatched energy. This is how we open ourselves to unhealthy relationships that push us into uncomfortable spaces. When you learn to be true to yourself, there will be no need to search for validation. It is time to take your power back!

While it may seem easy to tell another adult to respect your boundaries, it may be more difficult to uphold boundaries with your children. Children look to us for their basic needs, but this doesn't stop us from teaching them certain standards they must follow. We must remember that children learn from us by imitation. They are sponges who soak all the information around them. When you place proper boundaries, it teaches them how to speak up for themselves as well. If we can admit that much of the healing we are completing is directly connected to our childhood experience, then we can understand the importance of parenting with purpose. The idea that your inner child has suffered due to your parent not having the tools may be true.

But the adult version of yourself is responsible for correcting these learned behavior patterns. A generational curse is a learned behavior pattern that negatively affects your family passed down from one generation to another. You must ask yourself whether you are willing to continue being a prisoner of your fears or break free by claiming the life you deserve. Fear and faith cannot reside in the same space. Do you have faith in yourself that you can live a well-lived life, or will fear continue to paralyze you from being the change you deserve to see?

11 Signs of Healthy Boundaries	11 Signs of Unhealthy Boundaries
Own your time	Struggle with low self-esteem and have a critical inner dialogue.
Prioritize time for self.	Often feel too advantage of
High self-esteem and self-respect	Feel guilty for expressing boundaries.
Set limits for others without feeling bad	Fear of backlash from standing in your power
Create a strong sense of identity and direction	Create a strong sense of identity and direction
Able to say no and stand firm in your decision	Share space with people who don't align with you for fear of being alone
You clearly state your wants and needs	Take on other people's problems as your own
You take care of your needs.	Stay in unhealthy situations, thinking you can change someone else.
You understand you cannot save others from themselves	You put other people's needs before your own
You have a strong sense of direction and are not seeking validation from others.	You tend to become burnt out by commitments and responsibilities that overwhelm you.

The

re are five types of boundaries:

- Physical focuses on your personal space, your privacy, and your body.
- Financial focuses on your spending habits. Are they helping you to achieve your financial goals or causing more stress?
- Intellectuality focuses on your thoughts and beliefs. Do you allow yourself to have negative self-talk? Do you allow others to silence your voice when you are expressing yourself?
- Emotional focusing on how comfortable you are with expressing your feelings with others.
- Sexual focuses on your expectations concerning intimacy.

Clear boundaries should be established and communicated effectively. When you feel your boundary is being challenged, it is important to assertively communicate your needs. This also necessitates maintaining a high level of consistency to ensure a smooth flow. To assist you in identifying your focus, let's address a few questions.

- What types of things make you feel replenished?

_____
_____
_____
_____
_____

- What activities in your day do you dread?

_____
_____
_____
_____
_____

- What do you look forward to the most?

_____
_____
_____
_____

- What makes you feel valued, safe, and supported?

_____

_____

_____

_____

- What causes you discomfort or stress?

_____

_____

_____

_____

Next, I want you to draw a heart on a blank piece of paper. Inside that heart, place anything that brings your joy and makes you feel stress-free.

- Your family
- Love language
- A certain part of your routine

- Communicating effectively with the people you love
- Freedom to spend your time how you wish

Next, draw a square around the heart. Inside this square, write down anything that causes you emotional exhaustion, stress, or anxiety.

- Someone dictating how you should spend your life
- Working countless hours without taking time to care for yourself properly
- People sliming you with all of their problems
- Being touched without your permission
- Worrying what others think of you
- Your family not respecting your self-care time

The things in the square are items that you may want to set clear boundaries from, which will allow you to remove those feelings of exhaustion and stress. The heart represents things that keep you aligned more with your goal.

SETTING A FOUNDATION FOR SELF-ESTEEM

Self-esteem is something parents help children instill within themselves. We do this by teaching them the language of love. The way that we speak to our children reflects how they will value themselves. This also challenges us to look within and re-establish our own values of self-esteem. Ask yourself, do you speak to your children or at them? When speaking to a child, they need to feel heard. You do this by:

- Giving them your undivided attention
- Getting on their level
- Giving eye contact
- Practicing active listening
- Empathize and Validate feelings

Fostering self-esteem in children requires us to teach them to speak a new language. This is what we call the language of love. We show our love in different ways. Most are familiar with the 5 love languages: acts of service, quality time, physical touch, words of affirmation, and receiving gifts.

While we often apply these to our romantic relationships, they can coincide with any relationship.

Every family member receives love differently, from the oldest to the youngest. Love is shown based on the type of relationship you have with that individual. What I have found to be one of the most important for myself after the loss of my parents was words of affirmation. I equated so much of my worth to making my parents proud of the person I was becoming that when I could no longer hear them speaking life into me, I began questioning whether life was worth living. When that basic need was removed, I lost myself. We don't realize our basic needs' importance until they are removed. This sends us into survival mode, scrambling to replace whatever is missing. **Remember: There is nothing missing, and you are not broken.**

When starting a family, your job is cultivating an environment allowing them to grow with or without your presence. By teaching them to speak life into themselves using affirmations, you teach them a love of self. When you know who you are and what you're capable of, the love you have for yourself will overflow. This is something that can't be taken away by anyone or anything. Affirmations are a great way for you to begin this journey. You and your family should create expressions that are specific to each of you and several that can be related to your family or your family mission.

Previously we spoke about expressions of love compared to learning a new language. Being fluent would require you to practice daily until they become part of your routine. Before going out into the world and encountering different energies, recite your affirmations with your child during their morning routine. Tooth brushing time is perfect. They can already look at their reflection as they speak these powerful expressions of love to themselves. **Below write 4 affirmations you will repeat to yourself every morning.**

_____

_____

_____

_____

_____

CHAPTER 2

Taking your power back

Evaluating Your Stress

Rate each on a scale of 1-5. 1 being the least stressful and 5 being the most stressful.

- Worrying about your child's development 1 2 3 4 5
- Having enough food to eat 1 2 3 4 5
- My health 1 2 3 4 5
- Credit cards and bills 1 2 3 4
- Not enough money to pay bills 1 2 3 4 5
- Not having a good relationship with my co-parent 1 2 3 4 5
- Not having a good relationship with my parents 1 2 3 4 5
- Buying things, I can't afford 1 2 3 4 5
- Feelings of depression/ anxiety 1 2 3 4 5
- Not being able to calm my anger 1 2 3 4 5
- Not being able to handle my anxiety 1 2 3 4 5
- Fear that my family will interfere with my goals 1 2 3 4 5
- Losing friends who no longer align with me 1 2 3 4 5
- Not having a stable living environment for myself / my family 1 2 3 4 5
- Feeling attractive 1 2 3 4 5

- Feeling alone 1 2 3 4 5

- Differences with family values 1 2 3 4 5

- Fear of being hurt 1 2 3 4 5

- Fear of being wrong 1 2 3 4 5

- Fear of losing my dreams 1 2 3 4 5

- Fear that my children are being exposed to stress 1 2 3 4 5

- Not understanding my child's emotional needs 1 2 3 4 5

Circle any responses where you scored a 4 or 5. These items can become triggers to heighten stress situations. Below evaluate ways to work through and release.

1. When did the stress begin?

_____

_____

_____

_____

_____

_____

2. How does this stress impact you and your family?

_____

_____

_____

_____

_____

3. When faced with one of these stressors are you able to balance out your emotions effectively or are you reactive?

_____

_____

_____

_____

_____

_____

4. How do you feel when you are experiencing this stress? Ask yourself if this feeling is serving you or hindering you from accomplishing your goal.

_____

_____

_____

_____

_____

_____

5. Often when experiencing these situations, we become lost in emotions instead of focusing on a solution to our problem. Problems often arise to teach us a formative lesson on how to move forward in future scenarios. Take a moment to review your list of stressors. What are some positives you can identify from each scenario?

_____

_____

_____

_____

_____

_____

6. When you display signs of stress do you notice a change in your loved ones behavior? Do you ask for assistance from your family when you are feeling stressed?

_____

_____

_____

_____

_____

7. Asking for help can be extremely difficult for someone who is overcoming superhero syndrome. We convince ourselves that we can do it all alone or that we will be let down when we ask. What are some of the stories you have created that have hindered you from asking for help?

_____

_____

_____

_____

_____

8. What were the long-term effects of you not changing how you handle stress?

_____

_____

_____

_____

_____

_____

9. What will be the benefits of reducing your stress?

_____

_____

_____

_____

_____

_____

10. What are some barriers you have encountered when removing your stress?

_____

_____

_____

_____

_____

11. What do you need to avoid to reduce stress?

_____

_____

_____

_____

_____

12. Break down the top 3 stressors you rated on your stress scale.

1) The stress I want to release

_____

What are the causes?

_____

_____

_____

What level of stress do these items cause? (High, med, low)

What are some skills you possess that can help you solve this problem?

1_____

2_____

3_____

2) The stress I want to release

_____

What are the causes?

_____

_____

_____

What level of stress do these items cause? (High, med, low)

What are some skills you possess that can help you solve this problem?

1_____

2_____

3_____

3) The stress I want to release

_____

What are the causes?

_____

_____

_____

What level of stress do these items cause? (High, med, low)

What are some skills you possess that can help you solve this problem?

1_____

2_____

3_____

REFLECTION

Below take a moment to reflect on the topics you have covered. What were some of the things that triggered an emotional response from you? How will you follow through with this self-awareness in the future?

_____

_____

_____

_____

_____

_____

_____

_____

_____

_____

_____

_____

IDENTIFYING NEEDS

Each of us has basic needs that must be met for us to move in harmony. When one of them isn't being met, we become unbalanced. This seems to place us in survival mode, sending us in search of something to satisfy this need so that alignment can be restored.

Below make a list of your needs, make a list of your basic needs and ways to help maintain these needs.

Here are a few examples:

- Basic needs (food, water, warmth)
- Need for affection
- Need to belong to a group
- Need for self-esteem
- Need to feel safe
- _____
- _____
- _____
- _____
- _____

REMOVING ANGER

When parenting yourself, learning what emotion you are battling will allow you to become unstuck. Holding on to this emotion can have crippling effects. In this section, you will identify ways to process your anger.

- Is there something you are currently angry about?

_____

_____

_____

_____

_____

- Who or what is the cause of your anger?

_____

_____

_____

• Are you unhappy with your current state of living? What would you change?

_____

_____

_____

_____

_____

• Is there someone you feel has let you down? How has this impacted your relationship?

_____

_____

_____

_____

_____

_____

Now that we have covered anger let's review our responses. How many of them are directed at an outside source? While someone or something may have played a part in each scenario, only we have the power over how we respond to our emotions. As I stated previously, life is meant to bring forth challenges simply to test the tools we have been given. It is our choice to react or reflect on what is being presented. Our power is held in our ability to choose. Think of how much energy you spend when arguing with someone. By the time you have finished, your body is tired, you're drained, and you have nothing left to give yourself or others.

What if you held on to that energy by staying calm and evaluating ways to solve the problem? This technique may seem far-fetched, but it is extremely possible. As a behavior therapist, I have worked with numerous children with severe behavior diagnoses. I was responsible for teaching them how to communicate effectively without using aggression. While we have had countless moments where behavior has been displayed, I have found that the less attention I have given to it will cause it to diminish at a much higher rate. This is where our goals and values play a major role. While remembering these goals may seem difficult when heightened situations occur; I can tell you it gets easier with practice.

During this process it is imperative to be intentional with setting your standards forward. Anger is an energy that requires immediate attention. When we lack accountability for our emotions, they can seem overwhelming. Acknowledge this feeling and let it go by remembering what your goals are. Do not allow your emotions to rule how you operate in this space. You are in control. Take your power back by releasing what no longer serves you.

SELF HEALING AFFIRMATIONS

While looking at yourself in the mirror,

(State your name) I'm proud of you for _____.

(State your name) I forgive you for _____.

(State your name) I commit to _____.

I am _____.

I am _____.

Steps to Handling Your Anger:

- **Stop** before you say something hurtful and can't take it back
- **Communicate** that you need to take a break from the current situation
- **Take a break** and approach the situation later with a level head
- **Breathe** (We often don't realize that we hold our breath when we are upset. Counting may seem elementary, but each number stated out loud forces air into your lungs.)
- **Comprehend**: Ask yourself is this a big problem or a small problem
- **Establish a connection**: Empathize with the other party
- **Problem Solve**: Discuss different ways you and the other party gain clarity.
- **Mend:** Accountability and make plans on how to move forward.

ACCOUNTABILITY

Over the years of listening to parents speak about their hardships during their parenting journey, I have found a few common factors. The most common is making the decision to discipline by using conscious parenting or control. Most of us come from a generation where children were seen and not heard. We weren't allowed to question the things that went on in our home. We were expected to follow through without much explanation.

Unfortunately, that has not proven to be the most successful. In fact, many of us have spent countless years searching for the answers we should have been given in childhood. It's clear that many of us have wanted to use an alternative form of parenting but haven't been sure how to apply the tools. We have all been children before and can resonate with our children's emotions; we must be willing to place ourselves in their shoes. We find it so easy to identify with the stories attached to our childhood traumas, but we are not willing to see that we sometimes use the same parenting style that has left us scared.

The first step to releasing Superhero syndrome is to accept your role in your own helplessness. Superhero Syndrome began in childhood as an attempt to please those in authority around you. We were taught never to question the authority figures in our homes because there were physical consequences. When I felt my mother's temperament was off, I would do anything to quiet the situation and not bring attention to myself. I recall each time she became upset with me; I never knew how she would react. There were times when I would be physically punished or ignored for hours or days at a time as I begged for her to speak to me or even acknowledge my presence. This led to me replaying the same scenario over and over, attempting to figure out where I had gone wrong and how I could mend what was broken. There were never any conversations about correcting the mistakes, only about the consequences. While working through this, I discovered that although I may have done something that did not align with the standards of my family's home, it was up to my parents to communicate appropriately and work together on how to move forward from these situations. We often become upset with others based on them breaking an expectation we may have set for them. It is not the responsibility of anyone to live up to our expectations. This mentality only leads to resentment and unnecessary disappointment. When we understand that each person is responsible for upholding their values and beliefs it is easier to release the idea that someone has purposely done something to make us upset. The reality is that no one has the power to make you upset. It is a choice to allow yourself to become moved by anger the very same way it is a choice to be moved into a joyous space. This is why setting goals and values with our children is such an important part of setting a proper foundation for expansion. When these behaviors are consistently reinforced, we are planting positive seeds to growth for the future.

The assumption many parents make is that their child understands how to display the correct behavior when they are still learning what they can do. As adults we can agree that many of the mistakes we made as children, did not warrant the responses that were given. Many times, outside forces had caused our parents to become overwhelmed and they often projected these emotions onto us. Although this may not have been intentional, it set the foundation for the way we view love from the most important people in our lives.

Over the years, after realizing I had endured physical and emotional abuse just like many others, it felt normal. Everyone seemed to share a similar childhood story. We accepted that this was just a part of our community and culture. Some of us, like myself, vowed that we would never subject our children to the same treatment.

Although we wanted change, we lacked the proper tools to guide us along our journey. We are still finding ways to cope with the emotions from our childhood and that has kept us stagnant. We become stuck due to us still resonating with the wounds of our past. I recall conversing with someone who told me they were struggling with their parents respecting them as adults. They said that they couldn't disagree with their parents without them either lashing out or removing communication. It made them question their self-esteem and shrink themselves. I wanted them to examine what they knew was true from the situation. I asked this person, who was in their late 30's at the time and residing in their own home with their children, why they had chosen to still allow this behavior to rule them? I also asked if they still identified with the child who was forced to endure this behavior? They stated they were not the child in their story. I then asked who they felt was responsible for their current feelings and if they had taken their power away by force? They decided they were allowing themselves to become triggered by their experience. They had allowed their stories to guide them well into their adulthood and it was now being projected onto the relationship not only with their children but with their spouse. When we state there is nothing we can do to change the outcome of our situation, we identify with powerlessness. Despite being unhappy with our current way of life, many of us decide it is much easier to stay in a familiar situation instead of accepting the part we have played in our own misery and navigate towards a healthier reality.

This is where learning to advocate comes in. It is our job to speak up for ourselves. We have spent so much time allowing our voices not to be heard for fear of losing out on something. We have become comfortable being victims of our own powerlessness. Speaking up for yourself should never affect your bond with someone. This only happens when they are comfortable with you aligning with powerlessness. Speaking up for yourself shows the importance of your boundaries. People will be forced to respect your choice to not align with things that no longer serve you or your purpose. This change can make people uncomfortable. This is not a time to become frustrated; instead, understand where the energy comes from. This also opens the door for proper channels of communication to be established. Most of us don't truly understand what healthy communication looks like because we are used to being talked at instead of talked to. We were also taught that children should never speak out and oppose adults, which made communication one-sided.

Children learn from what they experience. This simply means that children learn to communicate emotionally, verbally, and physically directly from their environment. This is where many of us still struggle to find balance in how we react when our life places us in what we consider a stressful situation. During childhood, much of the trauma we endured was not a choice. We were not in a space to care for ourselves and still needed to look for our parents or caregivers to satisfy our immediate need for safety and shelter. How these figures fulfilled this role directly affected how we have maneuvered through our lives. Although this set the foundation for how we have developed, we must make a choice to continue with the same pattern or learn something that will have a different result in the future. We must make a conscious choice on whether we want to be the victims of our past or the victors of our present. Although this may be part of your past, it does not belong on this path. We must take time to learn how to disconnect from our stories and stand in our power to build a strong foundation for our future. We do this by learning to take accountability for our role in our own pain.

When accepting accountability for yourself, you are taking ownership of the roles you have played in your life. It is extremely easy to point fingers at the individuals who have contributed to your story. This can also provide validation for the times when you were genuinely a victim, especially during childhood when you lacked the power to protect yourself from traumatic events. As we transition into adulthood, we are faced with two choices. We can choose to become powerless or make a change to create the reality we seek. When you point at an individual to place blame, there are three more fingers pointing back at you. This is when we must ask ourselves, what part did I play in creating this reality? You are no longer able to use your parents as an excuse. We can identify what feelings we no longer want to experience and do something about them. When we consciously choose to take no action toward change, we victimize ourselves again. Accountability allows you to identify and remove behaviors that no longer serve you. By doing this, we are also building a foundation for how your family will mirror your actions. Again, children learn what they live. So, by learning to take accountability for our actions, we are engraving these same values in generations to come.

Many of us have learned to move in this way for years, only surviving the things life has thrown at us. It is now time to live the life we have dreamed of. It is time to take responsibility for our mistakes by acknowledging them and actively taking steps to change your behavior. Children need to hear that the adults in their lives can admit when they are wrong and see them putting action to their words to change future results.

Accountability Self-check:

Answer each question based on your most recent experiences. Use these questions to help direct you through each activity.

• Do you become eager to learn from others? How do you incorporate the knowledge you have learned from others into your everyday life?

_____

_____

_____

_____

• Do I spend more time procrastinating or pushing myself to complete tasks?

_____

_____

_____

_____

- Do you envy other people's success? What do you feel you are lacking when comparing your success to others? What can you do to align with your goals moving forward?

_____

_____

_____

_____

_____

_____

- Do you spend more time complaining or working? What can you do to change the way you perceive your day to make it more enjoyable?

_____

_____

_____

_____

_____

_____

- Do you live an entitled life, or are you motivated to earn your own way? What steps can you take to elevate yourself to the next level?

_____

_____

_____

_____

_____

_____

- Do you tend to point fingers or problem-solve? What ways can you elevate your mindset when problem solving to see more success?

_____

_____

_____

_____

_____

_____

_____

- Do you encourage and praise your family and friends or are you more critical of them? How can you show more gratitude for those in your life and the space you share with them?

_____

_____

_____

_____

_____

- When life doesn't go your way, do you blame others for the emotions you are experiencing, or do you identify how to solve them effectively? What type of plan have you written down on how to achieve this goal?

_____

_____

_____

_____

_____

_____

- How often do you allow others' opinions of you to affect the way you view yourself? What ways can you practice speaking life into yourself daily?

_____

_____

_____

_____

_____

_____

- Do you make excuses for others' behavior? What boundaries have you put in place to assure your needs are being mutually respected?

_____

_____

_____

_____

_____

_____

- Do you stay in unhealthy situations and blame others for how they have made you feel? What boundaries or values have you put in place with those you care about to limit this behavior?

_____

_____

_____

_____

_____

_____

- Do you focus your energy on trying to change others behavior or mentality? How can you refocus your energy on evaluating the spaces you allow yourself to share with others?

_____

_____

_____

_____

_____

_____

FACE YOUR FEARS

Mirror work is a great first step to start moving towards the results you seek. Mirror work is an unorthodox way to practice connecting with your inner being by speaking life, love, and light into yourself. It is a great way to openly express the things you have been waiting for others to tell you. This is an opportunity for you to create affirmations and even open conversations with yourself on building a stronger version of yourself. When in survival mode, we often don't take the time to acknowledge our reflection. We are often hiding in plain sight, too ashamed to look ourselves in the eyes for the things we've allowed ourselves to tolerate. This is because we know we deserve more than we have accepted. We often become so attached to the identities that we have created that we no longer recognize the person looking back at us. Mirror work allows you to be vulnerable with yourself by taking off the veil you have worn for the world to cover up your authentic self. We often look at our reflection, basing our feelings on the superficial version of ourselves we show the world. We critique how we look based on how the world will judge our appearance, praying they don't see the broken pieces of ourselves we've tried to keep covered.

With any practice, to see results, you must be consistent in working on it daily. Each morning when you rise, you are given a new opportunity to start your day with new intentions to set the tone for how you visually see your day playing out. Are you ready to commit to a healthier version of yourself? You must be willing to show up for yourself like no one has ever done before. The tools in this book will only be helpful if you are willing to do the work. Understand that when completing this task, you may experience emotions as you acknowledge parts of you that have been hidden for some time. It is part of the way we release the energy that no longer serves us. I encourage you to take time to journal how you feel when seeing yourself for the first time.

- Schedule 2 mins you can dedicate to this activity
- Find a quiet place that will allow you to not be interrupted
- Stand in front of your mirror, staring into your eyes,
- Observe your breath
- Watch your chest go up and down

Choose or create affirmations that are specifically geared toward your journey. Affirmations are used to battle the negative talk and stories we create. Stating them out loud regularly reminds us of our goal and realigns our focus.

Ex: **I am worthy of love. I am enough. I am whole. I am loved. I am worthy of love.**

Another key component of affirming is identifying what you want to release. **Each statement will begin with your name.**

Examples:

_____ I release negative self- talk and will instead choose words that motivate me moving forward.

_____ I release any negative thoughts that will distract me from achieving my goal.

_____I am no longer holding on to the stories I created blaming others.

In our society, we have become resistant to change, wanting to continue moving in the same patterns because it is what was deemed normal. Why are we so resistant to change?

We allow ourselves to make continuous excuses for why it is easier to remain powerless. Change requires you to put in work to shift your consciousness. It is you embarking on a path you have never been on. The fear of the unknown can play a role in you naturally wanting to align with what you know to be familiar, even if it has caused a certain level of pain. In your subconscious mind, you know you've been able to survive your past. The question you must ask yourself is, are you ready to live in the present and thrive in the future? Life doesn't have to be painful. It is filled with experiences that are presented to help you learn valuable lessons. It is your choice to evaluate them and apply whatever lesson from the situation to future scenarios.

WALKING IN TRUTH

Learning to move from the adult version of yourself and not your inner child is the gateway to limiting excuses. We use the term inner child to describe the part of us that aligns with the child-like version of ourselves, especially the parts of us that experience trauma. We must understand that your inner child is present but should not be the one with the navigations to our lives. Once we have decided to live in the present, our inner child must take a backseat because it is not needed to operate from a space of wholeness. Our inner child has an unbalanced way of maneuvering in high-stress situations because it lacks the proper problem-solving tools. It cries out for attention instead of learning to communicate its needs effectively. You have all that you need and lack nothing. In the section identifying your needs, we recorded our basic needs. We must understand that when we give ourselves the power to speak freely and openly, the universe fulfills our needs in ways we could have never imagined.

Superhero syndrome forces us to identify from spaces of lack instead of abundance because you don't see it as possible. Your trauma tells you that because the adults in your childhood let you down, you must now complete every task yourself. This causes a delusion about how we can have healthy relationships with others.

Our ego or pride can hinder us from asking for help in stressful situations. Superhero Syndrome allows us to move from a space of protection where we convince ourselves that our advice is always the best even when we know we've had no experience in certain topics. This is how we set ourselves up for failure. The help is often right in front of us, but instead of reaching out or speaking up, we hold things in, allowing ourselves to become overwhelmed and burnt out. Parenting your children or reparenting yourself isn't a journey meant to be done alone. It is meant to be done with a village behind you. We convince ourselves that asking for help is a sign of weakness when in all reality, it's a sign of strength.

Many entrepreneurs enter their path to financial freedom with the idea that all the work must be done alone to achieve the ultimate financial reward. For most of us, we know the first year of business is the most trying because we are balancing out ways to pour into our business and find a sense of harmony. We often expect and desire instant rewards for the efforts we invest, which can make us hesitant to form partnerships in our business. We rob our business of the time we can spend bringing forth new creative ideas, trying to do everything alone. Therefore, we speak of cultivating an environment to allow you to thrive. Having a strong support system is imperative to reach your goals.

How often do you use resources? Are you comfortable asking those around you for help when you need it? I've heard many parents say they would rather struggle than ask their co-parent for help with their child's needs. Your pride can be the killer of all things that bring forth life. It forces you to often operate in a survival mood instead of a place of abundance. Are you tired of moving this way?

When I was introduced to the term superhero syndrome, I began thinking of my father. I often blamed him for not being able to connect with me emotionally. I was filled with so much anger and often resentment for his inability to support me. Once I began removing the stories, I had believed for so many years, I was able to identify what he was struggling with. A young boy who was a victim of child abuse, who witnessed his father beat his mother with no mercy, was forced to become the provider for 10 brothers and sisters. He was never allowed to live his life for himself. After speaking to individuals who were able to bear witness to his internal struggle, they stated he was sad and searching for guidance. He knew how to provide and did an excellent job doing so. However, he had no idea what communicating effectively or displaying healthy emotions looked like. Many individuals whose job is to provide for their families tend to place their needs on hold despite experiencing burnout, resentment, and exhaustion. They fed the narrative that everything would fall unless they continued to support these unrealistic and self-made expectations. I never considered that I was projecting my expectation onto him when he lacked the knowledge that would allow him to move differently. He expressed moments of his own anger and resentment towards himself and others for the decision to stay instead of walking away and live his life the way he saw fit.

We each have a duty to evaluate whether we are walking in truth or choosing to align with stories. Some of our parents had rough upbringings and may not have had the proper tools to teach proper communication or emotional regulation. But what is also true is that we can continue fueling that narrative or write our own. We are responsible for giving the next generation a strong foundation so that they can live well with or without us.

We must remove our judgment and stories attached to our childhood experiences to show more empathy for those who came before us. We are not asking you to discredit your experience but to simply understand that trauma makes or breaks how an individual functions, especially when they don't have the proper tools or support. With your knowledge, are you capable of withstanding your power to change your family's story? In this book, you will be provided with several diverse ways to guide you as you build a solid foundation for yourself and your family.

TRANSPARENCY CHECK

1. When was the last time you felt yourself becoming overwhelmed by your responsibilities as a caregiver or parent?

_____

_____

_____

_____

_____

_____

2. What are 4 steps you can take to pour into yourself when these moments occur?

_____

_____

_____

_____

_____

3. Were there times that you resented your decision to put others first in your life? How did you release this feeling?

_____

_____

_____

_____

_____

_____

4. What boundaries can you put in place to help you maintain a sense of harmony?

_____

_____

_____

_____

_____

"To build a solid foundation for yourself and family you must have discipline, dedication, effective communication, and empathy. These are all components of you moving with the intention to reteach yourself a new meaning to love of self. "

Whitney Gilbert

Repeat this statement.

"I am taking charge of my life; I am letting go of self-pity and sadness over being treated badly as a child. It is only as hard as I allow it to be. I identify as the adult version of myself by reminding myself of what I know to be true. I am no longer in a helpless space. When I identify with helplessness, I am moving farther away from living in a state of wholeness. My inner child can no longer dictate how I move through life. It is only a reminder of my strength and perseverance in the past. I am focusing my energy on moving with love and truth. I will be kinder to myself by replacing negative self-talk with affirmations that align with my actions. There is nothing broken inside me. I am whole. I am love. I am Light.

Listed below are examples of positive words and affirmations. Use any that resonates with you in your daily practice.

- I'm willing to take care of you
- I love how thoughtful you are
- I am worthy of love
- I am enough
- I am exactly who I need to be at this moment
- I will use my fears to fuel me
- I am doing the best I can every day

- I love how unique my body is
- I accept that life has problems, and I will deal with them.
- I am beautiful
- I am whole
- I know its ok to ask for help
- I love embracing my fears
- I am fierce and strong. I trust my intuition
- I am open and receptive

SPEAKING LIFE INTO YOURSELF

Speaking life into yourself is a way to replenish your energy. When learning any foreign language, it will take time for you to become fluent. You will need to practice this new language daily so that it flows freely without you thinking about it. You may also surround yourself with people who are fluent in the language you are learning. This allows one to practice this language often until it becomes natural. Learning to speak life into yourself works the same way.

In this section, list 10 things you wish you heard more often from the people in your life. What are some things you need to hear? Once identified, practice saying each to yourself.

1._____

2._____

3._____

4._____

5._____

6._____

7._____

8._____

9._____

10._____

TAKING ACTION - Watering your Garden

I want to ask yourself how you want to be remembered. We now know that our children are reflections of us. How can you help them build a strong foundation? You do this by cultivating an environment that reflects the results you want to see. I sit with my plants as a gardener, speaking life into them. With every breath I take, they inhale the carbon dioxide my body releases. I use organic soil and compost to strengthen and water the roots regularly. This is the same process you complete with your family. They are your garden! It is your duty to nurture the seeds you have been sent so that they can have the strength to flourish for multiple seasons. A certain level of discipline, intention, and acceptance is necessary when tending to your seeds. Consistency in fulfilling their basic needs is essential to ensure their growth.

CULTIVATING YOUR ENVIRONMENT

Cultivating the environment you need to help you and your family achieve your end goal

List 5 People you consider close to you

_____

_____

_____

_____

_____

List the people who make you feel supported.

_____

_____

_____

_____

_____

What type of energy do they encompass?

_____

_____

_____

_____

_____

List 3 adjectives to describe how you feel when you talk to this person.

1. _____

2. _____

3. _____

Do they take your feelings and needs into account?

_____

Do they tell you tough truths when you need to hear them?

_____

Do they celebrate your triumphs with you?

_____

Do your values align?

_____

Do you consider them role models?

_____

How can these individuals better support you in your life?

Often, we can easily identify what we want from others but can't identify what others should expect from us. We have learned it's easier to place blame on other individuals instead of taking accountability for the parts we played in breaking our own hearts. Most of our support isn't effective because we set unrealistic or unvoiced expectations. When selecting a support, it's imperative that you can reflect on what you are asking of others as well. Be true to yourself when selecting. Do your responses line up with your support?

RATE YOURSELF ON A SCALE OF 1-3.
1 - YES, 2 - SOMETIMES, 3 - NO

DO I APOLOGIZE WHEN I'M WRONG	1	2	3
I TELL THE TRUTH	1	2	3
I JUDGE OTHERS WHEN THEY MAKE MISTAKES	1	2	3
I STAND BEHIND MY VALUES	1	2	3
I SHARE WITHOUT ATTACHED CONDITIONS	1	2	3
I MIRROR THE BEHAVIOR I WANT TO SEE.	1	2	3
I LISTEN WITHOUT JUDGING	1	2	3
I FOLLOW THROUGH WHEN I COMMIT MYSELF TO SOMETHING	1	2	3

IDENTIFY YOUR SUPPORT SYSTEM

We are surrounded by different forms of help and resources. Unfortunately, when the help we seek doesn't come in the form we envisioned, we overlook its possibilities leaving us to experience unnecessary stress and anxiety. We create stories that allow us to feel like we are alone when life gives us challenges when we have extensive resources at our fingertips. If you cannot find a solution to your problem, you must create one.

Now think about places outside of your home. Can you identify extra support systems? Ask yourself if your support systems were unavailable who would you call upon?

Name 10 people and places you can find help when you need it. List all possibilities (family, internet, community, friends)

1.

2.

3.

4.

5.

6.

7.

8.

9.

10.

RATE YOUR SUPPORT SYSTEM ON A SCALE OF 1-3.
1 - YES, 2 - SOMETIMES, 3 - NO

THEY APOLOGIZE WHEN THEY'RE WRONG	1	2	3
THEY TELL THE TRUTH	1	2	3
THEY JUDGE OTHERS WHEN MISTAKES ARE MADE	1	2	3
THEY STAND BEHIND THEIR VALUES	1	2	3
THEY SHARE WITHOUT ATTACHED CONDITIONS	1	2	3
THEY MIRROR THE BEHAVIOR THEY WANT TO SEE.	1	2	3
THEY LISTEN WITHOUT JUDGING	1	2	3
THEY FOLLOW THROUGH WHEN THEY COMMIT THEMSELVES TO SOMETHING	1	2	3

E

VALUATING YOUR DAILY TASK

List a daily schedule starting from the time you wake up until you turn in for the evening. Be sure to schedule time for yourself as well as.

_____

_____

_____

_____

_____

_____

_____

_____

_____

CHAPTER 3

Building Your Foundation

In your role as a parent, your job is to help your child cultivate the environment that allows them to flourish. You are a contractor hired by the divine to use your knowledge and life experience to bring this new being's creations to fruition. The first step to doing this is by releasing the idea that you are the owner of this being you've been gifted. In this relationship, you are working to build your child a strong foundation with the lessons you teach them over the years. Just like a building, the foundation is the most important because it dictates how long a structure can withstand the natural elements sent to weaken it. When parenting with purpose, your foundation consists of your values. Your family. This is how you cultivate the environment you seek. In this section, we will discuss effective ways to communicate.

COMMUNICATING EFFECTIVELY

Communication is crucial for establishing and sustaining healthy relationships. We rely on communication to express our desires and address issues we wish to eliminate. For instance, when setting boundaries, it is essential to effectively articulate them with clarity, rather than providing vague explanations. While communication during moments of joy may present its own challenges, the real test lies in effectively communicating when problems arise. This is when effective communication becomes highly significant.

Many of us come from a time when a child's opinion was minimized over the adults in their lives. Children were not allowed to oppose or question why they were experiencing certain things. Instead, we were told to be quiet and go with the flow. This ideology causes individuals to feel invalidated and often feel powerless. This can have two adverse reactions. One would be a person growing up and still allowing their voices to be unheard or someone who invalidates others to gain a level of control to make up for what they lacked. Conflict often enhances survival mode making us reactive instead of looking at ways to respond appropriately to the problem being presented. This is why practicing effective communication is essential.

Below is a list of statements related to communication. Place a check next to any that represents how you presently engage during communication.

- I perform another task (cleaning, on social media, watching TV, etc.) while listening to someone talk about something upsetting to him or her.
- I daydream while listening to someone express his/her thoughts or ideas.
- I will stop a speaker in mid-sentence to interject my opinion if I disagree with a statement.
- When listening to a speaker, I make eye contact.
- I will summarize the point of the speaker to ensure I have understood.
- I allow my mind to wander if a speaker doesn't engage my interest.
- I give my full attention if someone is talking to me.
- I make disapproving faces when I don't approve of what others are telling me.
- I find myself thinking about how I'm going to respond when the speaker is talking.
- People complain that I don't look like I'm listening when they

talk to me.
- I ask questions to encourage a speaker to elaborate on their point.
- Before I judge or comment on what the speaker is saying, I wait for them to finish speaking.
- When someone vents to me about their emotions, I wait until they have finished before I respond.
- I audibly groan or make another kind of disapproving sound when someone states something I disagree with.
- I interrupt when I have something to add to the conversation.
- I answer my phone during an important discussion.
- I finish other people's sentences before they have a chance to.
- I come up with different ways to escape conversations that don't interest me.
- I grow impatient when someone takes too long to get to the point.
- I don't want to engage when I'm not the one leading the conversation of controlling the pace.
- I closely observe the body language of a speaker when listening to them.

Tips to use when challenging conversations are presented.

When beginning any conversation, take note of the person's body language. Take time to ask them if they're ready to engage with you or if they need more time to process. We tend to feel extremely comfortable doing something I call "sliming" individuals we are close to with our stories and demands without asking permission before doing so. This tends to lead to undesired results. It is your job to build rapport with the other party.

- If you are speaking with a child, get on their level so that you can have direct eye contact to ensure they are listening. This is how you establish a connection with them. Remember, children can become distracted very quickly, especially when you ask them something they would prefer not to take part in. Use clear and direct language. This is a great time to use reinforcement to keep them focused on the result you seek.

- Summarize the point of the speaker to ensure you have understood.
- Ask the other party to elaborate if there is something you need clarity on.

- Avoid using accusatory statements, as this can cause the other party to become defensive, leading farther away from a solution.

WHAT I WANT FOR MY CHILD

Every parent has a picture painted in their mind of what they would want their child to be. This requires you to instill these skills within your child and consistently follow through. This can also be applied to other adult relationships you may have.

Below write several characteristics that you would like your child to possess. Then describe in detail how you can nurture this characteristic within your child.

1) I want my child to be

_____

To nurture this characteristic, I will

_____

2) I want my child to be

_____

To nurture this characteristic, I will

_____

3) I want my child to be

_____

To nurture this characteristic, I will

_____

4) I want my child to be

_____

To nurture this characteristic, I will

_____

5) I want my child to be

_____

To nurture this characteristic, I will

_____

Children are like sponges who absorb the energy and information provided from the world around them. We have been chosen as their first teacher to love and guide them while on their path to becoming adults. Our job as parents and caregivers is to teach our children how to communicate their needs by teaching them language. Everyone has their own basic needs that allow them to experience heightened joy. We all need to feel wanted, connected, respected, and safe. When any of these are missing, we begin moving out of harmony. This causes us to move into survival mode, causing stress or feeling overwhelmed. While we can identify clearly with these emotions for ourselves, we find it extremely difficult when our children mirror this very same behavior.

As humans, we all have similar needs; the way we communicate with others is the only thing that differs. When a child requires any of these items, they will display certain behaviors that will allow you to see something is wrong. They may throw a tantrum, call your name a million times, or simply ask you to play with them. They will not give up until that need is met in some way. They are extremely persistent. In the past, these behaviors may have triggered a physical need to redirect the child. This type of behavior shows individuals that punishment is the result of expressing a need. This teaches them to go without or seek fulfillment elsewhere. In such moments, we can use our power to focus on our values and align with our family goals. By choosing not to react to the behavior displayed, we can use one of the most important tools we have learned thus far, effective communication. In the upcoming section, you will go over examples of ways to effectively communicate boundaries, redirection, family values, and accountability by using realistic scenarios.

REINFORCEMENT, CONSEQUENCES, AND FOLLOW THROUGH

In the field of behavior therapy, I have learned the importance of reinforcement. If we think about this logically, we are all motivated by some outside source to follow through. We are less likely to complete the task when we don't prefer that reinforcement. For example, when we are at work, we are motivated to show up and complete a task based on our receiving a financial reward to compensate us. If there was no guarantee that we would be paid for our work, the likelihood of us showing up for work would lessen. Reinforcement helps us to feel validated. It helps us know we are doing great and makes us want to do more tasks that will give us this feeling. The same can be said for our children. We often expect them to follow through with tasks because "I said so" and don't allow them to understand the importance of the task or to be accountable for following through. Reinforcement helps us discover what items, tasks, or people our child is motivated by.

Children's most preferred reinforcement is being able to spend time with their parents for several reasons. It allows them to gain access to your attention and feel safe, which are some of the basic needs they require to feel balanced or in harmony. This is also why they struggle so much when they are separated from you. Verbal praises and using something tangible they can engage with are necessary as well. When working with children, there are several steps to help children gain access to reinforcement.

- Select an age-appropriate task. Do not set unrealistic expectations for them to complete a task independently when the skill has not been taught or you have witnessed them complete the task appropriately.
- Explain the task to the child and set expectations you have for them to follow through. Also, explain that when the task is completed, they will have access to reinforcement (Have them choose the item). State the importance of the task and how following through will be beneficial to their goals and family values. Use this as an opportunity to teach accountability. Have them restate the instructions back to you to ensure they understand the task in its entirety.
- Give them an opportunity to complete it on their own. This will differ based on the age of your child. If your child is just learning a

task, you may have to allow them to complete the task with you several times before they can complete it independently.

- If the task is completed, thank them for following through by giving them overwhelming amounts of praise or by receiving the tangible item. If the task is still not completed, ask questions. How can I help? Offer them a more effective way to complete the task.
- If the task was not done based on the child becoming distracted or due to them engaging in behavior that does not align with your family values, redirect by reminding them of what reinforcer they are working towards to help motivate them. This is a perfect time for you to explain how their choices to follow through can have positive or negative consequences. Do not allow their behavior to overwhelm you. Children have a much shorter attention span than adults, and when left alone, they can and will engage in other activities. They also will give pushback to see whether you are going to give in to their behavior. They are used to you doing things for them and are learning to grasp the idea of becoming more independent. By redirecting them, you are helping to shape their skill to stay on task for the future.

- Once the task is completed, give verbal praise and state that they have gained their reinforcer.

- If their task is not completed and you have received pushback from your child after redirecting, you can now explain how their choice not to follow through has not gained them access to reinforcement. This may cause additional behavior. If your child begins to tantrum, allow them to calm down. This does not mean leaving them alone. Children still require help to regulate their emotions. Often, they are overwhelmed with the changes and require physical contact to help them calm down. The best tool I put in place for my 5-year-old bonus baby was to give her the ability to ask for a hug during her tantrum. This allowed her to establish a connection with us while she calmed down. You can sit with them quietly. If your child is older, ask them if they would like to be alone while they calm down. Let them know you will be back to check on them.

- Once they have completely calmed down, ask what caused them to become upset. Children will not always see the part they play in the outcome of situations. This is where we begin teaching accountability.

- Ask them to state what the task was and what the expectations were when they started. If they don't remember, help them navigate. Allow them to state what they would receive if they completed the task and how their choice did not allow them access to that item. Discuss what choices they can make in the future that will help them obtain this reinforcer.
- During any of these moments, if you feel overwhelmed, take a step away to allow time to calm down. This is new for both of you, do not become discouraged.

Results will not happen overnight. Success is in the follow-through.

In nature, animals' bond with their children while teaching them essential skills that will help them gain independence and meet their basic needs. In a lion pride, the lionesses are responsible for teaching the offspring how to hunt to help feed their families. When they are unsuccessful, their entire family is at risk of going hungry. There is a natural consequence for the action. Although failed attempts happen, it allows the lion to use the tools it has learned to help them to better navigate in challenging moments. In the world of gentle parenting, there are mixed emotions attached to using consequences with children.

There is no perfect way for a family to function. Each unit must choose what works best for them. In my experience, children learn to become responsible by taking accountability for their actions. Once learned, this is a skill that is carried with them into adulthood, where they are to grasp the importance of following through and problem-solving effectively. Once your three steps are completed, your child may require additional explanation as to why the task was important.

Children need to understand that their choices will help them maintain balance in the future.

- Communicating effectively =removes high levels of stress
- Treating others with respect =creating a strong support system
- Completing tasks in a timely fashion = more time for self/ less risk for burnout
- A significant aspect of effective communication is keeping in mind that our objective is to ensure that the other party can truly understand what is being conveyed. This may necessitate meeting them at their level, allowing the child to feel at ease while expressing themselves without judgment or interruption. While it can be challenging to resist the urge to immediately solve a problem for your child, take a moment to remind yourself of the ultimate goal in this process.
- Remind yourself that if we want our children to make the proper choices independently, we must allow them to solve them independently. At times they may struggle with navigating through the conversation due to becoming distracted or not having the words to describe what they are experiencing.

This is a great time to offer help. We must remember that children who learn and practice these skills will become adults who have a strong foundation.

Think of times when you were attempting to express yourself but were constantly ignored or cut off by the other party when they felt the need to interject.

How did this make you?

Did you become frustrated?

Did it teach you to quiet your voice?

When individuals don't feel they aren't heard, they seek other ways to bring attention to themselves or make themselves small. There's is power in teaching your child that while I may not always agree with you, your voice is one to be heard. By listening to their needs, you are also opening a door for other meaningful conversations to flourish. This allows you to hear other ways they may need your guidance. While these skills can be used to help your children build a strong foundation for communication, they are also great for helping adults navigate through problems amongst themselves. Becoming a parent opens your eyes to the responsibilities that come with being directly connected with them. For those of us who are looking for ways to parent ourselves, these same skills are necessary for establishing a strong foundation for ourselves and experiencing a life well lived.

For many individuals who struggle with verbal expression, finding alternative outlets to release their energy becomes necessary. This may involve stepping out of our comfort zones and engaging in unfamiliar activities. When I faced challenges in articulating my emotions, I turned to writing, meditation, and painting. I allowed myself to visualize the colors that corresponded to specific emotions. For instance, I depicted anger with red on my canvas, and I repeated this process for other emotions like purple or blue. I also incorporated words that spontaneously came to mind. Engaging in creative endeavors, whether for children or adults, is an incredible way to process emotions. It doesn't require expertise, only the commitment to follow through with the task.

Sometimes when learning to communicate, we need to start with open-ended questions. Below is a list of questions to try with your family and friends.

What makes you happy?

_____

_____

_____

_____

If you could do anything right now, what would you do?

_____

_____

_____

_____

_____

_____

What makes you feel loved?

___

How do you show people that you care?

What does it feel like when I hug you?

_____

_____

_____

_____

_____

_____

_____

What do you enjoy giving people?

_____

_____

_____

_____

_____

_____

_____

What would make you smile a little extra today?

_____

_____

_____

_____

_____

_____

How do you best like helping others?

_____

_____

_____

_____

_____

_____

_____

What can we do to enhance the time we spend with one another?

_____

_____

_____

_____

_____

_____

Where in the universe do you want to go for a visit?

_____

_____

_____

_____

_____

_____

Who is your worst enemy, and why?

What do you want to be when you grow up?

What's your dream vacation?

What makes a good friend?

Describe yourself using positive I statements.

_____

_____

_____

_____

_____

_____

_____

CHAPTER 4

How Grief Can Trigger Superhero Syndrome

UNDERSTANDING GRIEF & OVERCOMING LOSS

One of the hardest periods of my life came to pass after losing my parents. Everything I thought I knew before their loss seemed to go out of the window. Even though I felt I was ready for what was to come, I was not prepared for the whirlwind of emotions I was going to experience. I deemed myself a strong individual who overcame plenty of obstacles and was always able to find a solution to any problem. Unfortunately, this unfamiliar territory knocked me off my feet. I found myself sinking deeper and deeper into a place of darkness.

Every individual has a different experience with loss. Three of the biggest components that dictated my experience were my support system, personality, and my coping mechanisms. Our personality will play a major role in how we process the experience. Ultimately it will determine the amount of drive we have to get through it. In each of our experiences, we must learn to shift our consciousness to adapt to our new life. This doesn't only happen with death but with any loss. What hinders many of us is our inability to lead with truth and instead we allow our emotions and stories to guide us. Emotions allow us to create stories as to why we did not deserve the loss or blame outside factors. Loss is inevitable, but many of us feel as though it is a choice. We don't get to choose our time in this space with others or the things life presents to us. The only thing we can control is how we can make the most of each day we are given.

There are no rules to this process except to allow yourself to go through the experience without a fight. I've heard individuals say they aren't ready to feel the emotions related to a loss, so they've tucked them away until they feel they can truly process it. While this may work for a short period of time, it will slowly leak into other aspects of your life subconsciously.

Many of us spend so much time running from the reality of our situations instead of discovering the lessons within. I recall a time in my mother's last days when she decided to stop herself from asking God to spare her. She said," How dare I feel exempt from this process? What makes me more special than anyone else that I shouldn't go through this experience? Why not me?" It was then that I was able to begin viewing loss differently.

Just like we experience the stages of grief when facing the death of a loved one, we also go through similar stages when dealing with other significant losses. It is possible to become consumed by the process of letting go and moving forward. When we find ourselves trapped in feelings of sadness or anger, it can have an impact on:

- Relationship
- Parenting or the energy to have to interact with your children.
- Health
- Work
- Happiness
- Self
- Setting goals for your future

IDENTIFYING THE STAGES OF GRIEF

The stages of grief include:

- Not wanting to accept what has already transpired.
- Shutting down
- Staying busy all the time
- Procrastination
- Anger
- Frustration
- Impatience
- Rage
- Feelings of being out of control
- Irritability
- Passive aggressive
- Bargaining
- Perfectionism=insecurity
- Thinking about what you should have or could have done
- Judgment towards self and others
- Ruminating over the future or the past =guilt

- Comparing self to others
- Overthinking and worrying=fear Depression:
- Sleeping habits change=sadness
- Reduced interest in socializing
- Reduced motivation
- Increase in alcohol and drug usage= ways to run from emotions
- Crying
- Acceptance
- Being present now
- Assertive, non-defensive, honest communication
- Mindful behaviors
- Accepting the reality of what truly is
- Able to be vulnerable and rationalize emotions. Loss can also bring on feelings of:
- Self-doubt
- Low self-esteem
- Make you physically sick.
- Cause your body and heart to ache.
- Intensified emotions

- Frightened
- Powerless
- Awkward
- Confused
- Embarrassed
- Exhausted

One misconception of grief is that it comes in linear stages, which is untrue. For most, these stages come in many different orders. Some may experience more than one at a time or even revisit the same stage more than once. Grief is also not synonymous with death. It can be experienced with any loss, such as:

- Loss of relationship (significant other, friendship)
- A normal family life
- Feelings of safety
- Homes or possessions
- Loss of health
- Loss of time
- Financial stability

- Plans/ dreams of the future
- Identity
- Freedom
- Independence
- Innocence

When experiencing any type of loss, you can easily become engulfed in your emotions and disconnect from your goals. This is how we get sucked back into survival mode. Survival mode allows us to abandon our new tools during problem-solving and instead resort to familiar tactics when emotions become overwhelming.

Superhero syndrome is a byproduct of our attempt to overcompensate for what we have lost. While this may be extremely difficult for us to navigate due to the intensity of the emotions we may be facing, we must not forget the power we have within us to work through these moments. While we must experience these emotions, we have the power to work through them and not allow them to take complete control of us.

Unpacking

Have you been stuck in any of these stages? If yes, which ones?

_____

_____

_____

_____

_____

_____

What about these stages continue to bring the most emotions?

_____

_____

_____

_____

_____

_____

What stages are you still dealing with?

___

What stages have you already overcome?

___

What do you feel you are lacking from this loss?

_____

_____

_____

_____

_____

_____

How has this process affected the relationships in your life?

_____

_____

_____

_____

_____

_____

What things can you change about the loss you encountered?

_____

_____

_____

_____

_____

_____

_____

If there is nothing you can actively change about the loss you have encountered, it is time to choose to move forward. This will open the door for new opportunities, but you must be able to receive what is being offered to you. Being stuck in this cycle allows us to put up a resistance to new possibilities. We become so focused on the loss that we resist what the universe is offering, causing us to self-sabotage our greatness.

ELIMINATING THE WHY

One of the hardest questions we ask when dealing with loss is, Why? We spin ourselves in circles trying to make sense of what we are experiencing while creating stories to support our failed expectations.

When releasing the aspects of superhero syndrome, we must allow ourselves to remove the whys.

We want to know:

- Why has the loss occurred?
- Why did it happen to us?
- What, not someone else?
- Why didn't I see this coming?
- Why did this happen now?
- Why didn't God stop this?

Our whys can lead to us becoming engulfed in anger. We can become resentful towards ourselves and others when we cannot see a clear answer to these questions. We must take the time to remove them to focus on living in the now and the goals we have set for ourselves.

On a piece of paper, write down any questions you have related to the loss you are experiencing. Ask yourself if they are helping you to align with your goals and values. If the answer is no, then you can determine they will not help you move forward. Once you have written them down, find a safe environment and destroy this paper. We must release what is no longer serving us or hindering our growth in any way.

While moving forward from a loss may seem strenuous, it can also bring forth new strengths within us. There is beauty in all that we experience, but it is our job to find it. Instead, we tend to focus on the things we have no power to change. There is always a lesson to learn from all the madness.

What are some of the positives you have experienced? List them below.

1. _____

2. _____

3. _____

4. _____

5. _____

6. _____

7. _____

8. _____

9. _____

10. _____

Made in the USA
Columbia, SC
21 March 2025